Original title:
Wind Among the Willows

Copyright © 2025 Creative Arts Management OÜ
All rights reserved.

Author: Lucas Harrington
ISBN HARDBACK: 978-1-80566-759-9
ISBN PAPERBACK: 978-1-80566-829-9

The Quietude of the Flourishing Grove

In the grove where laughter hides,
Squirrels dance with wobbly strides.
A raccoon juggles acorns galore,
While chipmunks argue, 'It's my turn to score!'

Pinecones drop with little 'thuds',
Frogs croak songs filled with 'nuds'.
A snail takes a selfie with a leaf,
Proclaiming this moment, 'Beyond belief!'

Tales Told by Shifting Sands

Sandcastles rise with kingly grace,
Only to fall. Oh, what a race!
Crabs scuttle off with a sly little grin,
While gulls debate on where to begin.

The tide giggles as it pulls back tight,
Whispers of stories that dance in the light.
A flip-flop flies like a jester's cap,
Leaving footprints in the laughter of sandmap.

Spirits of the Shimmering Stream

Bubbles pop like giggles in air,
Fish tell tales with a splash and flair.
A duck quacks jokes about a ducklings' show,
While turtles debate who can swim the slow.

Dragonflies flit with zany delight,
Wings shimmering, a marvelous sight.
A frog recites poetry in a croaky tone,
Concluding with 'Ribbit! I rule on my throne!'

Veils of Mist and Memory

Mist rolls in with a cheeky grin,
Hiding secrets of where to begin.
A fox pranks a deer with a sudden dash,
While owls share tales with a leisurely splash.

Shadows join in for a humorous play,
With laughter echoing through the gray.
A squirrel forgets where it buried its snack,
And memories swirl like fog, never slack.

Petals Adrift in the Calm

Petals dance on the streams,
As frogs belt out silly schemes.
A snail just slipped on a leaf,
His little face showed disbelief.

Birds gather for a raucous cheer,
While a lazy tortoise draws near.
The flowers wink with delight,
As crickets laugh into the night.

Beneath the Twilit Arch

Under a sky of cotton candy,
Glowworms giggle, a bit dandy.
A hedgehog rolls on his back,
Thinking up a daring snack.

The stars twinkle like fireflies bright,
While mice indulge in a dance tonight.
The breeze whispers jokes to the trees,
Tickling leaves with a gentle tease.

The Meadow's Gentle Embrace

In a meadow full of bliss,
A bumblebee gave a clumsy kiss.
Butterflies towed by the breeze,
Play tag over dainty cheese.

A squirrel juggles acorns galore,
While rabbits round up for a score.
The daisies shake their heads in mirth,
For this is the best kind of earth.

Currents of the Celestial Canopy

Under a roof of twinkling lights,
The owls are sharing funny sights.
A raccoon's got a cookie plan,
Dreams of a feast like a true champ!

The comical clouds wander and sway,
Like old friends gabbing all day.
While laughter floats through the air,
Nature smiles with a vibrant flair.

Mirth Among the Whispering Trees

In the grove where giggles play,
Branches bend in a silly sway.
Squirrels dance, they leap and dive,
Laughing loud, they feel alive.

Rabbits hop, with ears held high,
Chasing shadows as they fly.
Under leaves that crack and creak,
They share jokes, their laughter peaks.

A tortoise joins, slow yet spry,
Tells a tale of the clouded sky.
With every twist, the crowd roars loud,
Nature's stage, a jolly crowd.

So let's all join this merry chase,
Finding fun in every place.
In whispers soft, the trees will sing,
Of joy and laughter, oh what a fling!

Tales from the Softly Swaying Green

Grasshoppers chirp in rhyming twirls,
While the wind plays with the curls.
With every hop, and every skip,
Nature gives us a funny rip.

Bees are buzzing, full of cheer,
As they dance in the warm frontier.
Flowers chuckle, throwing shade,
At a bumbling bug, misadayed.

The frog's a joker, dressed in moss,
With croaks that always bring the gloss.
"Ribbit!" he says, then slips and slides,
His splash a laugh, as joy abides.

Underneath the mighty trees,
Tales of humor flow like breeze.
Laughter swells, a vibrant scene,
In stories spun from grass so green.

Hues of the Twilight Canopy

As dusk descends, the fireflies glow,
Painting swirls in a funny show.
The crickets laugh in syncopated song,
A pitch so high, where they all belong.

In the twilight, shadows bend,
With playful spirits that never end.
A raccoon pranks, a cheeky thief,
Stealing snacks, oh what a grief!

The owls hoot in playful jest,
With eyes a-whirl, they puff their chest.
"Who cooks for you?" the wise one mocks,
As laughter hops from branch to rocks.

In hues of dusk, whispers twine,
Crafting funny tales divine.
Underneath the canvas bright,
Their chuckles dance into the night!

Journeys Through the Verdant Glade

Come take a trip through leaves that sway,
Where funny creatures come out to play.
A pink-nosed pig on a leafy trail,
Telling stories that never fail.

A dapper mouse with pockets wide,
Shares his cheese with a grinning guide.
Through vibrant paths of leaf and vine,
Every twist is a silly sign.

The raccoons gather for a feast,
Making jokes about the least!
A turtle joins with a wobbly grace,
Carrying snacks in a slow-paced race.

With giggles bubbling through the air,
Adventures await, if you dare!
In the glade, where mischief reigns,
Laughter lingers, breaking chains.

Murmurs of the Forgotten Path

In the grove where whispers dwell,
Squirrels chatter, casting a spell.
A hedgehog sneezes, stirs the leaves,
And laughter echoes, as he grieves.

A turtle trips and starts to roll,
He claims it's fun, but it's not whole.
The rabbits snicker, dart and flee,
While crickets break into a spree.

A tortoise dreams of fast-paced games,
His friends just laugh and call him names.
But still he smiles, slow as can be,
Content to let the world run free.

In the end, it's all in play,
These silly friends enjoy the day.
With each brief pause, they share a jest,
Mirth brings joy, they know it best.

Secrets Beneath the Canopy

Beneath the trees where shadows loom,
A raccoon plots some grand costume.
He's gathered leaves to make a hat,
And winks at all who stop to chat.

The owls are wise, or so they say,
Yet fumble when they lose their way.
A chorus of giggles fills the air,
As they bump into branches, unaware.

Mice play tricks, hide tiny treats,
While weaving tales in rhythmic beats.
Each rustle holds a secret cheer,
As antics bubble, loud and clear.

The forest hums, it knows the score,
With whispers funny, it keeps the lore.
Against the bark, the laughter grows,
In every nook, a grin bestows.

Reflections in the Quiet Water

By the pond, the frogs have gathered,
To sing a tune that's slightly scattered.
With croaks that sound like birthday cheer,
They leap and dive without a fear.

A fish rolls over, dazed and sleek,
While lily pads provide a peek.
The sound of splashes fills the air,
A tangle of glee, no sign of care.

A duckling slips and starts to glide,
With wobbly feet, she takes a ride.
Her friends all quack and cheer aloud,
Embracing mishaps, feeling proud.

Reflections ripple, smiles abound,
In every splash, pure joy is found.
Around the pond, the laughter flows,
In quiet water, friendship grows.

The Dance of Dappled Light

In sunlit spots where shadows play,
The butterflies swirl, causing dismay.
A tweak of color, a quickened flight,
Brings giggles forth, a sheer delight.

A young fox prances, quite in style,
But trips and grins, stays in the pile.
While beetles rumble, marching by,
They'll never let a good fun die.

The fawns peek out, their eyes wide bright,
As sunlight dapples with sporadic light.
Each flicker hints at tales anew,
In this merry dance, a joyful view.

With every flap and every twirl,
Nature's humor begins to unfurl.
Amongst the leaves, the laughter rings,
In harmony, this wild heart sings.

Murmurs Beneath the Willowy Arch

Under the arch where whispers play,
The rabbits giggle, come what may.
A squirrel slips, with nuts in tow,
His acorn hat steals the show!

The breeze tosses leaves like confetti,
As frogs croak jokes while looking petty.
Each rustle hides a laugh or two,
While bees buzz by in their best hue.

A turtle jokes with his shelled friend,
'Why rush?' he asks, 'We've time to spend!'
The shadows dance like mischief's call,
In the archway's shade, we have a ball!

So come, let's frolic, let's not be coy,
For laughter flows and brings us joy.
Under the arch where silliness thrives,
Together we make the best of lives!

Whimsy of the Fleeing Shadows

Under the trees, the shadows glide,
Dancing around in glee, they hide.
A hedgehog twirls, a pie on his nose,
And giggles break out wherever he goes.

The sun plays tricks, its rays confound,
As ducklings waddle, with laughter profound.
They trip and tumble, so careless and spry,
Chasing their tails, oh how they fly!

A crow makes puns from the tallest pine,
His quips and caws are simply divine.
Each shadow that flees makes room for another,
An orchestra of giggles, sister and brother!

So let's join the game, just sprint and dash,
For in this hilarity, we'll make a splash.
With whimsy surrounding, our hearts set free,
We'll laugh with the shadows beneath the tree.

The Emphatic Pulse of Green

In the vibrant glade, oh what a sight,
Bumbling beetles debate day and night.
A lizard lounges with style and flair,
While flowers giggle, without a care.

The blades of grass whisper their charms,
As playful bumblebees flaunt their arms.
A ladybug twirls, a tiny diva,
Chasing her friends like a playful river.

Blossoms sway, making silly faces,
As critters gather in secret places.
With each pulse of green, a chuckle is born,
As joy narrates the tale we adorn.

So take a step in this lively scene,
Where laughter and nature form a routine.
With every leaf, let splendid fun reign,
In the vivid embrace of soft, gentle grain.

Harmony in the Heart of the Thicket

Nestled deep where the thicket hums,
A pickled owl rattles his funny drums.
Squirrels gather for a grand soirée,
To plot and plan their crafty ballet.

The bushes chuckle with every breeze,
As flowers toss petals with momentary tease.
The gophers cheer, in their muddy hall,
"We'll have a feast! Let's all have a ball!"

With each rustle, a new game comes alive,
As fireflies blink, their lights will dive.
The harmony sings of silly delight,
In the heart of the thicket, all feels right.

So come take a stroll through laughter's domain,
Where joy is abundant and never in vain.
In the thicket's embrace, we'll dance and we'll play,
Creating a symphony, day after day!

Serene Journeys Through Verdant Realms

In green patches, critters play,
Chasing shadows, day by day,
Otters giggle in their splashes,
While turtles groan in climbing crashes.

Mice in hats with tiny canes,
Sail the streams with silly gains,
Squirrels dance on acorn tops,
Giggling as the river drops.

Frogs in line for the best show,
Jumping high, and stealing woe,
They croak out lines like pros at night,
While fireflies provide the light.

With laughter ringing through the trees,
Nature plays as if to tease,
In every rustle, every shout,
A merry dance, there's never doubt.

Musing on the Swaying Thorns

Thorns in bushes whisper tales,
Of jaunty jinks and clumsy fails,
Bumblebees with goofy spins,
Buzz around, making silly grins.

A porcupine with prickly flair,
Tries to dance but fills the air,
With awkward moves, oh what a sight,
While hedgehogs cheer with pure delight.

Vines that twist and twine with glee,
Claiming each branch as royalty,
Beneath them, snails are sneaking by,
Their little homes, oh me, oh my!

Amidst the thorns, the laughter grows,
In every corner, joy bestows,
Those prickly beasts in drapes of green,
Create a scene both wild and keen.

Lament of the Lost Fern

A fern once bright, now gone from sight,
Wanders off into the night,
Sighing softly, it took a chance,
To find new roots, to learn new dance.

Laid on rocks, it hums a tune,
That tickles crickets 'neath the moon,
A heartfelt plea, for friends nearby,
"Join me, dance, or at least try!"

Its leaves like arms, stretched wide with hope,
Lost amidst the mossy slope,
But every whisper in the air,
Is laughter echoing, everywhere.

So ferns may roam and drift away,
While others frolic here and play,
In every breeze, a tale is spun,
Of loss and joy, all rolled in one.

The Stillness Between the Breaths

In quiet woods where laughter rests,
Ponds reflect the quirkiest quests,
A raccoon dons a bird-like mask,
Pretending it's a feathered task.

Squirrels pause, they hold their peace,
Listening to the nonsense increase,
They giggle low but can't resist,
The antics caught within the mist.

Bubbles rise where frogs convene,
To toast to days that once have been,
With every splash, a splash of cheer,
A whimsy party drawing near.

The stillness hums a silly tune,
While critters plot beneath the moon,
In the calm, they find their fun,
Where bright adventures have begun.

Whispers of the Meadow

In the field where daisies dance,
A rabbit wears a jaunty pants.
The snail races by, with glee,
Shouting, "Catch me if you see!"

Butterflies do acrobats,
While frogs pretend to be top hats.
The grass sings silly tunes at dawn,
And mole gives a yawn, then carries on.

A squirrel climbs with goofy grace,
He trips and falls right on his face!
With giggles shared among the leaves,
Nature laughs as the sunlight weaves.

The flowers gossip, their petals sway,
They tease the breeze to come and play.
In this meadow, joy abounds,
Where laughter hides in all the sounds.

Laughter in the Tall Grass

The blades of grass tickle their toes,
As bunnies hop and strike funny poses.
Beetles in suits perform a show,
While crickets serenade below.

A hedgehog rolls to steal the scene,
In a paper hat, looking quite keen.
The ants form lines, a parade on track,
Marching with rhythm, no one looks back.

The daisies wink at passing bees,
Who buzz around with cheerful ease.
In this playful patch, mischief's a must,
Where every creature finds grand fun just.

Squirrels toss acorns, flying near,
Landing atop of a deer's left ear.
Nature's comedy, a grand delight,
As the stars awaken, shining bright.

Secrets of the Rustic Grove

In the grove where the branches bend,
The silly woodpecker taps, my friend.
A chipmunk juggles acorns with flair,
While the timid owl just stops to stare.

The rabbits host a tea party feast,
Where every critter is quite the beast.
With cookies made of dirt and moss,
They laugh at how they always toss.

The frogs put on a talent show,
Ribbiting jokes, then off they go.
The flashes of laughter fill the air,
With secrets shared, without a care.

As shadows stretch and day turns black,
The fireflies join in the laughter pack.
In this rustic haven, joy shines bright,
Even the stars twinkle with delight.

Breezes in the Ancient Hollow

In the ancient hollow where echoes play,
The whispers of leaves have much to say.
A turtle in glasses reads a book,
While a fox peeks in with a sly look.

The trees chuckle as they sway,
At the playful antics of a stray.
A beaver builds a wobbly dam,
And falls right in—oh, what a jam!

The shadows wiggle, the light does dance,
As fireflies twirl in a sparkly trance.
A badger shares his favorite joke,
And even the stones begin to poke.

As night falls softly, the stars pop bright,
Creatures gather in the fading light.
In this hollow, laughter sways high,
With the echoes of joy that can't say goodbye.

In the Embrace of Whispering Grasses

In fields of green, the laughter flows,
As ticklish stems dance through our toes.
A game of tag with fluffy clouds,
While nature chuckles, lifting crowds.

The rabbits hop, a dizzy spree,
They giggle loud, just you and me.
With every breeze, a tickle stays,
In this silly, sunlit maze.

The flowers sway, in bloom's delight,
Sporting petals bold and bright.
While critters play an unseen hand,
Bringing smiles across the land.

So join the dance, let's take a chance,
With rosy cheeks, we skip and prance.
In whispers soft, the grasses tease,
As we share jokes with buzzing bees.

The Tryst of Earth and Sky

Above the trees, a cloud winks sly,
While raindrops tease as they zip by.
A glance exchanged, the earth's delight,
As laughter bubbles in soft daylight.

The daisies giggle, they know the plan,
To sprinkle smiles across the land.
With every bloom and twist of fate,
The jesters of nature play and create.

The sun peeks in, a shy parade,
While shadows stretch in sunlit shade.
Together they frolic, making a scene,
Where earth and sky are truly keen.

A tumble here, a tumble there,
With nature's pranks beyond compare.
In this sweet jest of skies and ground,
The joy of life is always found.

A Lament for Fleeting Moments

Oh, fleeting time, how you slip away,
Like a rascally fox at the end of the day.
We chase the sun, it's all in fun,
But shadows grow long, and day is done.

The giggles fade as twilight calls,
While fireflies light up nighttime halls.
We treasure the laughs, in echoes we keep,
As dreams flip and flop, diving into sleep.

Yet every tick of the clock brings cheer,
In every moment, laughter's near.
With every sigh of the passing breeze,
We share our joys with giggling trees.

So here's to moments, both silly and sweet,
In their fleeting ways, they can't be beat.
We'll laugh out loud, come what may,
In the dance of time, we want to play.

Echoes of the Enchanted Glade

In the heart of the woods, there's a tale to tell,
Of whispers and giggles where all creatures dwell.
A frog croaks chorus, a tuneful croon,
While fireflies twinkle, under the moon.

The mushrooms giggle, their caps in a whirl,
As brambles shake hands, a prickly swirl.
The hedgehog rolls in a belly of glee,
While the owls hoot softly, setting beats free.

With every leaf that flutters and flaps,
The woodland bursts forth in raucous claps.
A festival wild, everyone's here,
With nectar to sip and nothing to fear.

So come take a step in this magical place,
Where joy wraps around you like a warm embrace.
In echoes of laughter, all creatures unite,
Let's dance through the glade, till morning's first light.

A Symphony of Leaves

Rustling whispers, leaves at play,
Swaying gently, night and day.
Squirrels dance, a clumsy show,
In their nutty, rhythmic flow.

Laughter echoes through the trees,
Tickling branches in the breeze.
A raccoon hums a silly tune,
Underneath the laughing moon.

Pine cones tumble, soft and round,
While chipmunks prance upon the ground.
Nature's jesters, free and bold,
Creating stories to be told.

In this frolic, joy ignites,
A grand concert of funny sights.
Leaves applaud with rustling cheer,
As laughter rings from far and near.

Tranquility Beneath the Celestial Dome

Beneath a sky so wide and bright,
Frogs play banjo, what a sight!
Dragonflies in bow ties glide,
As crickets cheer, they're filled with pride.

Turtles sport their sunburned shells,
While rabbit jokes are told in spells.
Here the sounds of laughter soar,
As every leaf becomes a chore.

The stars above are twinkling eyes,
While fireflies compete in size.
A celestial comedy unfolds,
In this tranquil space, joy molds.

When nature laughs, it's pure delight,
Underneath the starlit night.
So come and join this merry roam,
In the laughter of the earth, our home.

Whispers Through the Thicket

In the thicket, secrets peek,
Squeaky voices make us squeak.
A fox in sneakers makes a dash,
While owls giggle, what a clash!

Rabbits trade their carrots bright,
Giggling at the funny sight.
Nuts are flying, squirrels shout,
Playing games that twist about.

In this corner, laughter swells,
As hedgehogs tell their funny tales.
Everyone is in on the fun,
Creating joy for everyone.

So if you wander through the green,
Listen close, 'tis quite a scene.
For nature's jesters roam this land,
In playful antics, ever grand.

Dance of the Dappled Leaves

Leaves are twirling, feeling spry,
Lizards leap, and frogs can fly!
Every branch a dancer grand,
Nature's party, close at hand.

The sunlight plays, a gentle tease,
As shadows giggle in the breeze.
A bumblebee with tiny shoes,
Encourages the flower's blues.

Every rustle adds a beat,
As nature's rhythm lures our feet.
Here, the world is filled with cheer,
In every rustle, laughter near.

So come and join this leafy spree,
In the dance of pure glee!
As colorful leaves sway and twirl,
In this merry, dappled whirl.

Tales from the Treetops

A squirrel in a top hat, quite the sight,
Dancing with the breeze, oh what a flight.
He twirls and he spins, with acorns in hand,
Critters laugh aloud, it's a sight that's grand.

The owl gave a hoot, in a voice so sly,
Said, "Raccoon, don't steal, or you'll surely fly!"
The raccoon just winked, with a grin too wide,
"No need for a broom, I'm already a glide!"

A hedgehog in boots, out for a stroll,
Tripped on a pebble, then rolled like a ball.
He declared with a chuckle, "Now isn't this fun?
Who knew a small rock could turn me to run?"

As shadows grew long, they gathered for tales,
Of mischief and mishaps, with laughter like gales.
In treetops of laughter, they reveled all night,
For life in the branches is pure delight!

Murmurs of the Maple Grove

In the grove where the branches sway with glee,
A rabbit held court, like he was royalty.
With a carrot in hand, he commanded the crowd,
"Who here thinks bunnies can dance proud and loud?"

A chorus of cheers filled the air with cheer,
As a cricket jumped up, "Oh, I'll show no fear!"
He leapt with a flourish and landed with grace,
But slipped on a leaf, and went flying through space!

The turtles were watching, so calm and so slow,
Said, "We could win races, if only we'd go!"
But their laughter echoed, "What's the hurry, my friend?
Watching is just as fun, we can recommend."

Then someone suggested they all play charades,
And so with delight, their evening cascades.
With giggles and snorts, under twilight's glow,
In the maple grove's charm, they embraced the show!

Sunbeams and Soft Breezes

A lizard named Larry, so slick and so spry,
Said, "Watch me do splits, and I'll reach for the sky!"
With a wiggle and twist, he gave it a try,
But landed in mud, oh my, oh my!

While frogs in their chorus croaked tunes so loud,
Planned a big concert, oh, they were so proud.
Each note they unleashed made feathers take flight,
So the birds soon joined in, a symphonic delight.

A hedgehog with style wore day-glow shades,
Showed off his best moves, with some funky parades.
The dance-off took off, as the sun dipped low,
And laughter erupted as they put on a show.

With sunbeams and giggles lighting the way,
They danced 'til the stars skyward made way.
In a world full of joy, where silliness thrives,
Each creature found magic, where mischief arrives!

The Hidden Pathway Through the Glade

Along a small path, in the glade's tight embrace,
A fox and a badger were caught in a race.
The fox thought he'd win, with a confident wink,
But tripped on a root, and fell with a clink!

The badger just chuckled, "I guess I'll take lead,
Even if I'm more slow, I'll plant a good seed."
With a tip of his hat, he strutted and strode,
While the fox rolled and tumbled, with a fun little ode.

A hare joined the scene, with a hop and a twirl,
"Let's make this a party, I'll show you my whirl!"
With confetti made of leaves, they danced all around,
Until critters were laughing, what joy they had found.

With dusk settling softly on each tired face,
They finished the day with a warm, soft embrace.
For within the glade's heart, where giggles abound,
They found friendship and fun, in laughter profound!

Rustling Secrets of the Vale

In the hush of the glade, things giggle and sway,
Squirrels hold court, jesting all day.
With acorns like crowns, they dance and they tease,
Even the oak trees shake leaves with ease.

A rabbit with style hops right on a beat,
While hedgehogs in bow ties compete for a seat.
The fluttering butterflies, adorned like the best,
Join in the laughter, a furry little fest.

The bubbling brook chuckles with glee and delight,
As frogs croak their jokes 'neath the glow of moonlight.
Each rustle and murmur brings mischief anew,
In the vale of secrets, no one's ever blue.

So gather your friends and come have a laugh,
Nature's the stage for a comical craft.
With every soft sigh and each tickle of grass,
In this merry land, let your troubles all pass.

Breezes Beneath the Boughs

There's chatter of critters beneath leafy crowns,
As breezes invite them with giggles and sounds.
A raccoon with antics drops berries with flair,
Leaves dance around, like they leap in the air.

The bushes all whisper their silliest tales,
Of mushrooms in jests wearing colorful veils.
The light-hearted sparrows, in mischief, will soar,
Looping and twirling, they shout, "More and more!"

A badger skips by with a song in his heart,
While bunnies breakdance, performing their art.
The shadows beneath the tall sycamore sway,
As laughter resounds, it's a jubilant day.

So come take a stroll, let your worries just fly,
With breezes that tickle and tickle you, why?
In this playful haven, we'll all let loose,
Under boughs where joy finds its truest excuse.

Shadows in the Meadow

In the meadow's embrace, shadows jump and creep,
A dance of delight makes the sun's laughter leap.
The daisies are giggling, their heads all a-bob,
As the shadows throw parties, they just can't stop.

Beneath the sun's warmth, the grass grows so tall,
Where snickers of insects entice one and all.
The butterflies waltz, with a twist and a spin,
While ants, in a line, wear their best silly grin.

Oh, a hare plays a joke, hops about with a twirl,
And the wind, oh so clever, gives leaves a good whirl.
Each whispering breeze has a laugh to impart,
Frolicking shadows, the soul of the heart.

So prance through the petals, let merry times bloom,
In shadows of laughter, there's always more room.
Collect all the joy that this meadow can share,
And plant it like seeds in the warmth of the air.

Flight of the Embered Sky

At twilight, the fireflies take to the air,
With lantern-like glows and a mischievous flare.
They twirl like little dancers, all sparkles and zest,
Playing hide-and-seek, they shine in their quest.

The owls, in their wisdom, throw laughs in the dark,
While crickets compose symphonies, bright with a spark.
"Just one more joke," whispers a fox, with a grin,
As the stars come alive, with a twinkle and spin.

A rabbit, quite clever, imitates a crow,
While the wise old toad croaks, "Go on, steal the show!"
The breeze tells a story, a cheeky affair,
And the trees stretch their branches, all hearts laid bare.

So fly with the evening, let laughter ensue,
In this embered sky where all joy feels so true.
With each fluttering flight, share the night's delight,
Under curtains of starlight, we revel in sight.

Subtle Serenades Under Starlight

Squeaky frogs sing a tune,
Underneath the silver moon.
Twirling leaves, a nature show,
Dancing to the crickets' flow.

Rabbits hop with fervent glee,
Chasing shadows, wild and free.
The stars snicker, oh so bright,
At this frolicsome delight.

An owl hoots a clumsy beat,
While raccoons dance on two feet.
Whispers of the night combine,
In a laughter-filled design.

Jokes are shared by bubbling streams,
Where every glimmer sparkles dreams.
Underneath this playful sky,
The night hums with a joyful sigh.

An Ode to the Open Field

A floppy hat upon my head,
Chasing clouds, I dash ahead.
Laughter echoes, soft and sweet,
As my shoes fly off my feet.

A tumbleweed rolls by with style,
I can't help but grin and smile.
Grasshoppers leap in a race,
Jumping high, they find their space.

Picnics scattered, crumbs on the ground,
In every nook, joys abound.
A squirrel steals my sandwich fast,
As I laugh, he runs aghast.

Oh, the joys the meadows bring,
Even bees that buzz and sting.
With each frolic, I embrace,
The laughter found in nature's grace.

Breezes Carrying Secrets Home

Whispers glide on airy trails,
Fanciful tales in fluffy pails.
Mice debate beneath the trees,
As squirrel giggles tease the breeze.

A tumble down the grassy knoll,
A dandelion takes a stroll.
A sheepish smile from a shy hare,
Embarrassed gasps pollute the air.

The bravest winds play tag with ducks,
Ruffling feathers, oh what luck!
Chasing after wobbly flies,
While butterflies just roll their eyes.

Chortles rise when evening falls,
As crickets join the evening calls.
Secrets shared with cheerful hums,
Nature's laughter, joy it drums.

The Language of Fluttering Leaves

Leaves engage in cheeky pranks,
Whisper stories, fill the banks.
With rustling chatter, they confide,
Caught in breezes, giggles slide.

Sassy saplings wiggle low,
Bending just to steal the show.
A leaf twirls, a solo dance,
Just to give the sun a chance.

While acorns share their wild dreams,
The branches sway, or so it seems.
A playful gust gives them a shove,
And nature laughs, oh what a love!

Underneath the leafy boughs,
Each cheery chuckle draws us close.
In this place where joy is sown,
The laughter of the green is known.

Reflections on Rippling Waters

A frog hops past with quite the flair,
His singing voice fills up the air.
The tadpoles giggle, spinning around,
In suits of bubbles, they leap and bound.

The fish peek up, with prying eyes,
While dragonflies perform their ties.
"What's that splash?" a turtle would jest,
Just nature's way of having a fest.

A leaf slips down like a clumsy kite,
Spinning slow, what a funny sight.
The ripples giggle, laugh in the sun,
A dance of joy, oh wasn't that fun?

Then comes the heron, all serious and stern,
"Can't you all see it's my turn?"
With a blink and a flap, he stirs the scene,
Leaving all laughs in his moonlit sheen.

Secrets of the Shaded Dell

Under the trees where shadows play,
Squirrels gossip throughout the day.
"Did you hear what the owl said?"
"He's too wise to ever lose his head!"

The flowers nod with brightly painted hues,
While the brambles hum, tapping their shoes.
"Watch out for bees; they're always a buzz!
Last week they tried to take over the fuzz."

A caterpillar grins, munching on leaves,
Dreaming of wings, the trick he believes.
"I'll show them all my fine transformation,"
While ants march by in a bold formation.

The tree stump chuckles, "Oh what a show!
I've seen it all, as you might know!"
The dell embraces every whim and jest,
In this funny haven, we're truly blessed.

The Flutter of Nature's Breath

The butterflies flutter, what a silly spree,
Chasing one another, 'catch me if you can, see?'
A buzzing bee, joins in the game,
"Don't catch my wings! You'll ruin my fame!"

The grasshoppers leap, trying to dance,
With each silly twirl, it's a froggy romance.
"Let's leap to the left!" they collectively cheer,
Just in time, oh dear, here comes a deer!

The tulips lean close, whispering in glee,
"Did you hear how the willow laughed by the sea?"
The breeze sways softly, with cheeky delight,
Tickling the petals, oh what a sight!

As the sun sets low, all gather round,
Sharing stories where fun can abound.
Nature's a party, a cozy affair,
With giggles and jests floating in the air.

Song of the Whispering Branches

The branches sway to a breezy tune,
A concert of rustles beneath the moon.
The owls hoot in a rhythm so neat,
While crickets keep tapping their tiny beat.

"Are we famous now?" whispers a twig,
"I'm sure the tree next door won't dig!"
And the old oak laughs, "We've always been here,
With all of you branches, there's nothing to fear!"

A woodpecker knocks to beat of the show,
"Here's my audition; I'm ready to go!"
The leaves all clap with a rustly cheer,
"Bravo!" they shout, "You're our star, dear!"

The moon peeks down, twinkling so bright,
As stories and laughter fill up the night.
In this leafy theater, fun never parts,
With whispers and chuckles that tickle our hearts.

Rhythms of Life in the Untamed

Breeze tickles leaves, oh what a tease,
Willows sway and dance with ease.
Critters chat, gossip's a-float,
As I ponder their lively note.

Jumping frogs make quite a splash,
Silly mice dart, a dash for cash.
Nature's jest, no one can resist,
Laughing together, oh what a twist!

Squirrels chatter, tails in the air,
Accusing one another without a care.
The river chuckles, smooth and bright,
As all join in for sheer delight.

When sunlight fades, shadows play,
Life's a jigsaw in disarray.
Yet amidst the hum of playful glee,
We find our rhythm, wild and free.

Enchantment in the Verdant Whisper

Mischievous winds stir the trees,
Leaves giggle, flipping with ease.
A frog on a log, with style so quaint,
Practices leaps like an old-time saint.

Bunnies hop in a chase so sweet,
Around the flowers, quick on their feet.
With petals that tickle, they frolic about,
In this charming land, there's never a drought.

The sun peeks in, playing hide and seek,
While dandelions sprinkle, oh-so-unique.
Each turn holds laughter, each corner a jest,
In nature's playground, we're all very blessed.

So let us waltz through the verdant lanes,
Where spirits are light, and joy reigns.
Each rustle and whisper, a tale to unfold,
In this enchanted realm, both funny and bold.

The Sway of the Wandering Blades

Grass blades play, swaying around,
A merry world without a sound.
Dancing in rhythm, they lift and twirl,
As insects hum in a happy whirl.

A snail slides by, carries his home,
With a pace so slow, he's free to roam.
Butterflies giggle, so light on the wing,
In this breezy ball, they proudly sing.

The rogue raccoon joins with a cheeky grin,
Stealing sweets with a mischievous spin.
All the while the tall grass sways,
In this lively scene, we'll spend our days.

Laughter echoes where nature convenes,
In every corner, joy intervenes.
Life's a dance on this grassy glade,
With the sway of the blades, we've got it made.

Comfort in the Canopied Retreat

Nestled beneath the leafy embrace,
Squirrels chatter, keeping up the pace.
A cozy nook, where all creatures meet,
Sharing secrets, oh what a treat!

Mice make pillows from soft mossy beds,
While rabbits weave tales from their heads.
A gentle breeze rattles branches so small,
Echoing laughter—nature's own call.

Birds exchange tales from the high above,
With chirps full of mischief, laughter, and love.
In this haven, all strife is forgot,
As we revel in nature, a jolly lot.

When sunset paints skies with colors so bright,
We huddle together, the stars join the night.
In this canopied retreat, hand in paw,
Life's simple pleasures leave us in awe.

A Tapestry of Rustling Voices

In a glade where whispers play,
Laughter twirls and flits away.
A squirrel prances, quite absurd,
While birds chirp gossip, oh so blurred.

A hedgehog rolls with a comical sigh,
Tailors a suit, oh my, oh my!
With fiddles playing on daisies fine,
Each creature dons a bright design.

The rabbit hops, boasting so bold,
Of tales too tall, with antics told.
Oxeye daisies chuckle and sway,
As prankster pollen drifts away.

And as the sun dips low with grace,
All join in for a twilight race.
As shadows stretch, the fun won't cease,
In this madcap world, there's pure delight and peace.

Dance of the Sunlit Glade

Underneath the mighty oak,
Critters gather, jesting folk.
A frog in boots begins to dance,
While museful bees in tune do prance.

With twirling leaves and dandelion hats,
The raccoon's waltz beats like that.
A snail in shades, moves oh so slow,
While chirping crickets steal the show.

From muddy banks, a bold duck shouts,
Joining in, skipping about.
They form a line – a silly parade,
With every hop, the earth is swayed.

As shadows stretch in evening's light,
Their giggles mix with the night.
In frolicsome joy, they all hold hands,
In nature's revelry, laughter stands.

Nature's Soft Serenade

The trees hum soft, their leaves afloat,
While ants march in a leaky boat.
A lazy cricket strums a tune,
Beneath a lazy, dozing moon.

Amid the blooms, a ladybug feasts,
As butterflies twirl, the greatest beasts.
They giggle at a snoozing hare,
With dreams of hops and fluffy hair.

The brook burbles secrets to the air,
As frogs croak back a playful dare.
A mischievous breeze, oh, what a tease,
Plays hide and seek among the trees.

In twilight's glow, the laughter's spun,
A gentle feast, a day well done.
With stars awake, the night does shine,
Their wholesome fun is simply divine.

Chasing the Flickers of Dusk

When the fireflies begin to twine,
A hedgehog spins, tries to dine.
With bright little lanterns glowing near,
The night unfolds its whimsical cheer.

A toad takes bets on a nearby log,
While crickets share tales of the fog.
Beneath the stars, the laughter flows,
As shadows dance where the wild grass grows.

A merry band of critters begins,
With silly games and cheeky grins.
They dodge and weave in playful jest,
In this raucous revel, they're truly blessed.

With the curtain drawn, the night draws tight,
Their giggles linger, a pure delight.
As dreams take wing on the breeze so light,
Fun tales await in the dance tonight.

Revelations from the Rustic Pathways

A squirrel wore my hat, what a sight!
He twirled around, oh what a delight!
With acorns in hand, he took off with glee,
I chased after him, but he climbed a tall tree.

The frogs had a dance, they called it a 'toad'
They wobbled and jiggled, it was quite the road.
I joined in their jig, what a curious crew,
We giggled and croaked, and the sky turned blue.

A hedgehog insisted on playing the flute,
His notes were quite sharp, like a wild root.
The raccoons roared laughter, a hilarious cheer,
As the hedgehog blushed, we all filled with beer.

The sun set softly, without a single care,
As shadows danced lightly through the cool evening air.
With critters around, life's never mundane,
In this rustic retreat, joy is our gain.

Embrace of the Enchanted Hollow

A rabbit in glasses read books on a log,
"Why read in a hole?" asked a curious frog.
"Because, my dear friend, it's a marvelous tale,"
He winked and he smiled, "As bright as a snail."

The mushrooms were chatting, with caps all aglow,
They argued on colors, "I'm orange!" said Joe.
"Your orange is dull, like a faded old sock!"
They teetered and trembled, each toppled rock.

A badger was painting the leaves with some spray,
He said, "I'm an artist, just brighten the gray!"
The trees laughed so hard, their branches would sway,
As squirrels began to perform ballet.

At dusk, they all gathered for tea by the creek,
With biscuits and laughter, the night felt unique.
In the embrace of this hollow, where silliness reigns,
We toast to our quirks, and forget all our pains.

Serenity in the Shady Grotto

A turtle wore sandals, oh what a display,
"I'm faster than you!" he'd often relay.
But when he did crawl, it was slow as a snail,
With laughter and giggles, we filled up the trail.

The butterflies argued, which flower's the star?
"I'm clearly the best, see my beautiful scar!"
But one called out boldly, "I've colors that glow!"
They fluttered and debated, stealing the show.

A raccoon in pajamas snored under the trees,
While critters tiptoed, with grace and with ease.
They piled up his snacks, just to make him wake,
He sprang up in panic, a chaos to make!

With shadows now dancing and stars shining bright,
We laughed at the nonsense beneath the moonlight.
In our shady grotto, where laughter flows free,
Serenity's foolish, but happy, you see!

Footsteps on the Mossy Trail

On the mossy green path, I stumbled on a gnome,
He had a big beard and a marvelous dome.
"I'm lost!" he declared, with a wink and a grin,
"I thought I was going to meet my old twin!"

A snail with a backpack moved at a slow pace,
He offered me snacks, "Want to join in the race?"
I giggled a bit, "You'll win without doubt!"
As he nibbled his lettuce, I burst in a shout!

The trees told me secrets in rustles and sighs,
"They want us to dance," whispered one with bright eyes.

So we twirled and spun, what a whimsical spree,
With nature as our stage, so wild and so free.

When twilight descended, we sighed with delight,
In the magic of moments that felt just so right.
With footsteps of laughter, on trails made of dreams,
Life's a giggle fest, or so, at least, it seems.

Echoes of the Wandering Stream

A frog in a hat sings a tune,
With a skip and a hop, he'll be gone too soon.
The fish start to laugh at the sight so rare,
As bubbles rise up through the fresh, cool air.

A turtle on stilts gives a grand show,
With a twist and a turn, watch him go slow.
He winks at a snail with an extravagant flair,
While the dragonflies buzz in the sunlight's glare.

A squirrel with a bowtie tries to impress,
But trips on a twig, oh what a mess!
As laughter rings out from the reeds and trees,
The stream carries joy on the playful breeze.

In this happy place, all creatures convene,
With mishaps and giggles, they dance and preen.
Echoes of laughter ripple through the green,
As the carefree antics unfold and are seen.

Shadows in the Sunlit Lane

A hedgehog in shades rolls down the way,
With wheels on his back, he's ready to play.
He zips past the flowers, bright and bold,
While butterflies giggle at the sight to behold.

A rabbit eats carrots with elegant flair,
Alas, he drops one without a care.
The birds croon sweet songs in a comedic tune,
As the sun giggles down from the friendly moon.

A family of mice in a line so neat,
Imitate dancers on wobbly feet.
Chasing their tails, what a marvelous sight,
As shadows dance gently, all hearts feel light.

With laughter contagious, both near and afar,
Sunlit lane thrives under the bright star.
In the midst of the day, with shadows that play,
The joy of the moment won't soon fade away.

Songs of the Gentle Current

A duck with a banjo strums songs of the day,
While turtles all cheer in their quirky way.
The lilies sway gently in rhythm and rhyme,
Singing of adventures, both silly and sublime.

A beaver with style wears a sparkling crown,
As the fish in the stream all gather around.
With splashes and giggles, they join in a beat,
Creating a melody, oh, what a treat!

A crab plays the drums on a shiny old shell,
While the heron hums softly, it's easy to tell.
Nature's orchestra starts without a cue,
As creatures unite in a joyful debut.

In this chorus of life, harmony flows,
From the sprightly young minnows to the wise old crows.

Songs of the current make troubles dissolve,
With laughter and music, the heart can evolve.

Dances of the Leafy Spirits

In the branches above, tiny fairies prance,
They twirl and they spin, inviting a chance.
To join in their frolic, the critters below,
Participate gleefully, putting on a show.

A hedgehog on tiptoes gives a sweet twirl,
While a bashful old snail joins in with a whirl.
With a flick of his tail, a young fox leads the cheer,
Bursting with laughter, as friends gather near.

The leaves join the fun, rustling with glee,
Each sway and each swirl dictates jubilee.
As dusk blankets gently, the spirits take flight,
With a wink and a giggle, they vanish from sight.

In the heart of the forest, where mischief takes root,
Dances ignite, making laughter astute.
The magic of moments in nature's embrace,
Leaves us all smiling, delighted in grace.

A Tapestry of Feathered Songs

Birds in bright jackets sing so loud,
Chirping their tales, oh they're so proud.
With a flap and a hop, they dance on a line,
Shoulders of titmice, oh how they shine!

Squirrels with acorns, they join the display,
Chasing their shadows, in such a fray.
Their chatter is silly, their antics a treat,
Tickling our hearts with their nimble feet.

A thrush struts about, puffed up like a king,
While a finch finds a hat made from grass in the spring.
They squabble and bicker, yet all is in jest,
Each little creature thinks they're the best!

So gather, we giggle at nature's broad show,
As laughter like music begins to flow.
For in this wild ruckus, joy takes its flight,
In a tapestry woven with feathers and light.

Lullabies of the Gentle Green

In the shade of the trees, the leaves softly sway,
A chorus of whispers, come out and play.
Grasshoppers croon in a rhythmic delight,
While a bunny hops by, in the soft moonlight.

A frog in the pond claims it's the king of the stream,
Croaking and leaping as if in a dream.
Slugs slide on a stage made of dew and of dirt,
Wearing tiny tuxedos, it's all quite absurd!

The daisies all giggle with each gentle breeze,
They sway in a line, put your worries at ease.
The old tortoise chuckles at the squirrel's smart tricks,
Declaring the playtime is a clock's little fix.

So let's dance with the flora, let our worries go,
As the lullabies hum in the soft afterglow.
For in this lush realm, with laughter we swell,
Nature's own stories, oh how they compel!

Flickers of Sunlight in the Thicket

Amidst the thick bushes where sunlight peeks through,
A chipmunk plays tag with an old, wise blue jay too.
Their game of hide-and-seek, a comical sight,
As they bounce around, what a silly flight!

A beetle in shades struts like it's on a spree,
While ants line up neatly, as ordered as can be.
But oops! There's confusion; they bump and they crash,
Now which little bug gets to win the grand bash?

With petals as pillows, they settle for tea,
Discussing their battles in cozy esprit.
The flowers all giggle, they join with a sway,
In this sunlight-dappled, vibrant ballet!

So let's toast to the creatures, both big and small,
Who fill every moment with laughter for all.
In the flicker of sunlight among leaves ever bright,
Joy blossoms freely, pure and outright!

Forays into the Secret Garden

A hidden retreat filled with jests and delights,
Where bunnies in shades organize fun little fights.
They race 'round the tulips, all flash and all dash,
While snails slither slowly, not feeling the crash.

A hedgehog on roller skates zooms with flair,
Spinning in circles without any care.
The flowers all clap with petal-rimmed hands,
As the butterflies twirl with their magical bands.

In corners they giggle, the secrets they share,
As a cat naps nearby, with a soft, furry air.
They whisper of dreams and the things they may do,
Creating a mischief that's fresh and brand new!

So come to this garden, let laughter abound,
In the forays of fun where joy can be found.
Life twirls like petals on a playful spree,
In this secret retreat, come dance wild and free!

Glistening Ripples of Forgotten Tales

In the shimmer where the waters dance,
Ripples giggle, daring a glance.
Frogs wear crowns, they leap and tease,
While dragonflies buzz, making a breeze.

Silly voices come from the reeds,
Chortling secrets, planting the seeds.
Old turtles chuckle at fishy jokes,
While silly beams tickle the oaks.

A snail on a quest for the fastest route,
In a rhythm slow, but never in doubt.
His shell, a fortress, he proudly twirls,
As laughter flows from the giggling swirls.

Across the brook with a splash and a dash,
Creatures gather for a raucous bash.
With every splash and a merry cheer,
The tales of yore come alive here.

The Journey Home Through Twisting Paths

Through twisted trails with a skip and a hop,
A hedgehog hums, never wanting to stop.
Squirrels scurry with bits of their finds,
As mischief is hatched in their bustling minds.

A porcupine jests with quilly finesse,
Making the others giggle in excess.
The path wobbles like jelly on spoons,
As night dances in with glittering moons.

Lo! A raccoon dons a pirate's hat,
Claiming the berry bush, meow and splat!
All join in the laughter, a chaotic parade,
As reflections in puddles of laughter cascade.

But soon comes the dusk, pulling the day,
Their steps become wobbly, fading away.
In the moonlight, friendship glows bright,
As sleepy heads dream of their playful night.

The Nature of Elysian Oaths

In a glade where echoes spin tales of cheer,
The critters declare, with a chuckle sincere.
A pact of friendship beneath the bright sky,
Where laughter and mischief in twirls occupy.

The mice sing songs with a squeaky twist,
While canines dance, promises tryst.
Each leafy whisper holds a fun secret,
As nature giggles, not a care to regret.

With otters slipping on slippery stones,
And badgers tossing some colorful cones,
Every pledge painted with colors of glee,
In this woodland wonder, wild and free.

So let's not forget, as friendships grow,
The silly oaths we all bestow.
In the heart of the woods, our spirits entwine,
With laughter like petals on whimsical wine.

The Caress of Softly Falling Shadows

As the day bids farewell and shadows entwine,
The frogs in the reeds start their raucous dine.
Whispers of laughter play softly at night,
With crickets joining in, a whimsical flight.

In the twilight, a drowsy owl hoots,
While party raccoons don their silly boots.
With shimmery sparkles glowing so bright,
A playful parade, blissful in flight.

Even the stars giggle and twinkle, indeed,
As fireflies buzz with mischief to lead.
The path home is a jolly array,
Of giggles and twirls keeping shadows at bay.

So dance with the soft whispers of night,
Join the enchantment, twirl with delight.
For in every shadow, a story does leap,
With the caress of joy, we safely shall sleep.

Gentle Whispers of the Fading Light

The grass does dance with glee and cheer,
A little mouse has found a beer!
The bloated otter sings a tune,
While chasing shadows 'neath the moon.

A sleepy frog jumps with delight,
And nearly lands in someone's bite.
The crickets laugh in chorus bright,
As fireflies flicker, spurning fright.

The Lull of the Leafy Sanctuary

The leaves are tickled by a breeze,
A squirrel giggles, feeling free.
A hedgehog rolls, all snug and tight,
While planning pranks for the night.

A lazy cat just snores and yawns,
Dreaming of fish on distant lawns.
The robins chatter, making fuss,
As twilight creeps on little bus.

Silent Wishes on the Filigree Air

The butterflies twirl in the air,
Playing tag without a care.
A rabbit lifts his tiny paws,
To join the fun without a flaw.

Mice sketch dreams upon a leaf,
While frogs mock birds with comical grief.
The whispers of grass tickle and tease,
Encouraging waltzes among the trees.

The Poetry in Nature's Whimsy

A toad sings verses quite absurd,
In hopes to woo a passing bird.
The willow sways with laughter proud,
As clouds gather, forming a crowd.

A raccoon's antics steal the scene,
Grabbing snacks, oh what a dream!
The moon smiles down with such delight,
As all join in the playful night.

Secrets Wrapped in Green

In leafy lanes where whispers play,
The tales of mice chase fears away.
They plot and scheme beneath the boughs,
In secret meetings, they take their vows.

A hedgehog dons a tiny hat,
With wild ideas, he plans a chat.
A frog jumps high with leaps of joy,
While laughing at a clumsy coy.

The sparrows gossip, flapping wings,
About the latest feathery flings.
"Did you hear what the snail found?"
"No, but let's twirl and spin around!"

Each rustle shares a silly tale,
Of muddy paws that leave a trail.
So join the dance of joyful cheer,
Where chaos reigns, and fun is near.

The Harmony of Flitting Shadows

On twilight paths where shadows prance,
The critters gather for a dance.
A badger spins, a rabbit twirls,
As laughter floats like merry swirls.

The dance floor's made of moonlit grass,
Where silly antics come to pass.
With nimble feet, they sway and slide,
While silent stars watch from their ride.

A field mouse juggles berries bright,
While fireflies glow with pure delight.
A squirrel drops, but bounces back,
With somersaults that steal the track.

With every hop and every twirl,
The evening smiles, a joyful whirl.
So let the night bring giggles round,
In harmony where fun is found.

Echoes of a Forgotten Path

In hidden trails where laughter's found,
Echoes bounce with a silly sound.
A tortoise struts, his shell so proud,
While silly songs drift through the crowd.

The bushes quake, a secret host,
With hedgehogs playing musical toast.
Each note a giggle, each chord a cheer,
As woodland friends gather near.

With acorns tossed in cheer and fright,
They play their games until the night.
A raccoon drapes leaves like a cape,
Defining wrong turns with each escape.

Like whispers lost in playful glee,
They sing the truth of harmony.
For in this woodland, joy resounds,
And echoes of laughter swirl around.

The Embrace of Soft Echoes

Beneath the trees, where shadows play,
Soft echoes tickle, inviting to stay.
A family of ducks in line so neat,
Waddle and quack to a comic beat.

A rabbit hops with ears so tall,
While mice imitate with a tiny sprawl.
The elder owl, wise and stout,
Chuckles at all, "What's this about?"

With every rustle, a secret shared,
Of acorn treasures and being unprepared.
The fawn trips over roots unseen,
And laughter erupts, pure and green.

So join the dance of soft delight,
Where echoes embrace the starry night.
In this merry place, joy flows so free,
A tapestry woven in whimsy's decree.

Echos of the Wandering Stream

In the shade of the trees, something rustles,
A raccoon with a hat, oh, what a tussle!
He fumbles for berries, it's quite the sight,
A dance of delight in the soft morning light.

A frog sings a tune, oh so out of tune,
The crickets just laugh, under the full moon.
With a hop and a plop, he joins in the spree,
A chorus of giggles from the old maple tree.

An otter on skates, what a wobbly show,
He drags his best buddy, they twirl to and fro.
Splashing and laughing, they shift in a whirl,
Who knew the stream had such fun ways to twirl?

So gather your pals, take a leap, take a jump,
For nature's just waiting, don't sit with a slump.
Enjoy the soft sounds, let the laughter bubble,
In the playful heart, there's always some trouble.

Serenity in the Swaying Grasses

The daisies are dancing, a silly ballet,
While ants hold the ropes in a grand cabaret.
A grasshopper leaps, with his top hat askew,
He bows to the daisies, it's quite a hullabaloo!

The wind bends the stems like a comical breeze,
A squirrel jumps in and gets stuck in the leaves.
He fumbles and tumbles, his pride in a tangle,
While the daisies all giggle and gently dangle.

A worm in a tux, he's the life of the party,
Twisting and twirling, a marvelous smarty.
The ants raise their glasses, all in wooden thimbles,
Toasting to the friends in the grass that wiggles.

Oh look, a cloud, can you see it go by?
It puffs like a marshmallow up in the sky.
The grass grows so tall, they could whisper a tale,
Of all the fine antics of the windy trail.

The Lullaby of Leafy Canopies

The branches sway gently, a lullaby hum,
Where chipmunks do tap-dance, oh, such a drum!
A squirrel in a mask plays peek-a-boo chase,
His acorns are hidden, they've all lost their place.

The leaves start to giggle, a lighthearted cheer,
As a bee with metal shades buzzes around here.
He fumbles his pollen, oh what a disaster,
Yet somehow he smiles, making nature much faster.

A snail with a snail-mail, slow mail to declare,
Writes letters to flowers and sends them with care.
The daisies reply, "We'd love a surprise!"
With petals all fluttering, they dance at the skies.

The sunbeams poke fun, through the bows they will peek,

They chuckle and giggle, playing hide and seek.
In the leafy embrace, nature shines bright,
Where laughter and joy form a whimsical light.

Tranquility in Twilight's Embrace

As dusk settles softly, a cat takes a stroll,
On the path paved with daisies, his eyes like coal.
He stops to smell flowers, in a funny old way,
Twirling his whiskers, inviting some play.

A hedgehog appears, rolling all in a swirl,
Becoming a ball, oh, what a wild twirl!
The moon starts to chuckle from high overhead,
As the critters all gather, driven by thread.

The twilight brings whispers, of secrets so sweet,
Time for a giggle beneath tiny feet.
With shadows that play, they dance come what may,
In the soft fading light of the end of the day.

So bring out the snacks, for the nighttime parade,
A banquet of laughter, a feast that won't fade.
Under stars that just wink, with a joyous embrace,
Nature laughs on, with a funny face.

www.ingramcontent.com/pod-product-compliance
Lightning Source LLC
Chambersburg PA
CBHW071847160426
43209CB00003B/443